FROM THE
TRENCHES OF

THOMAS BLANDFORD

PAGE PUBLISHING, INC.
New York, NY

First originally published by Page Publishing, Inc. 2016

ISBN 978-1-68213-180-0 (pbk)
ISBN 978-1-68213-181-7 (digital)

Printed in the United States of America

DEDICATION

I dedicate this book to the only true one who was actually with me through it all. He loved me when I felt hated and rejected. In fact, his words to me were, "Never will I leave you or forsake you." He was my warmth in the freezing cold, he was my best friend and still is, and he was my strength when I was weak and scared. He was bravery when it all seemed dark. He was my light. He is my savior, my king, my Lord, my God. Psalms 139:8 says, "If I go up to the heavens, you are there; if I make my bed in the depths/ hell, you are there." Nobody but nobody gets the highest praise or the most thanks, and I thank him and will do my hardest, my very best to God Almighty and his son Jesus Christ. The best freedom and victory does not come from money but in knowing him. God, to you, I give all thanks for those you put in my path to help me and my family and you in setting me free! Physically, mentally, spiritually, emotionally and financially. If you don't know Jesus, get to know him as he wants to do for you what he had done for me. Never mind the so-called church people or religious people. Jesus is all you need. I promise you that. To God be the glory!

****

My second dedication is to my dear mother. Even as I write this dedication, it brings tears to my eyes. My mother raised not only her own kids but others as well. She tried so hard to keep the house in order. She loved me even when I was unlovable. She was sick with multiple sclerosis, but she loved. She cooked, she cleaned, and she did our nappy heads. She loved unconditionally. Whether I failed or succeeded, she loved. Mother once told me, "The reason I live, Thomas, is for you." My mother was not only willing to sacrifice for us but also she was a sacrifice for us! She was the epitome of motherhood. She gave to those bad friends of mine when they were hungry. She would discipline me when she felt it was needed, even one time chasing me over a fence with a stick. My mother's name to me is the name of a saint. I think without her example of true sacrifice and true love, I may not have made it. I love you, Moms, and thank you so very much for teaching me to never be ashamed of who I was and for loving me even when I acted like the devil. You are my hero! I hope you are proud of me now.

****

I dedicate this to my good friend Don. You are my friend, my confidante, my ace, my man. There's not enough I can say about you. It's been more than twenty-eight years, and we are still best friends. You supported me through my marriage, my divorce, the drinking, the drugging. You were there when I was homeless. You would always tell me that you loved me, that things would get better, and you were there for me. You used to tell me something that I used to love hearing when I was young, "No matter what you do in life, Thomas, no matter how bad it's going to be, I'm always going to love you. I have no conditions on my love for you." I've never heard a guy talk like that before without thinking he was gay. But it made me happy to know someone loved me like that even if I never told you. I am sorry for the time I picked you up and threw you on the floor. I was in such a dark place with the drugs, yet you said, "I still love you. I'm going to keep praying for you." I feel so proud to call you my friend. I admire the fact that you turned down teaching positions in prestigious schools to help those who need you the most. I am proud of Excel, your nonprofit school, because you help people like myself, people coming out of prison, people who have trouble with drugs and alcohol, people off the streets. You go above and beyond what any other teacher would do. Lastly, thank you for allowing me to come to Massachusetts with you because knowing what happened to those who stayed behind in New York, I truly believe my life would've turned out completely different.

***

I thank God for putting a Jewish man who went to college and who studied music on the different side of the tracks. Thank you, Neil Lipson. Neil has helped me in a lot of ways. When I'm down, he picks me up. He's a part of my life. He's not only just a business partner, but he's a dear friend. I love Neil with all my heart. He's become part of my family. He's a character, but he's definitely a great man and a great saxophonist. He helped me fall in love with music again. Music that is missing today and that music really takes me away when I'm stressed. Neil has been an integral part of my life. I'm sure God has another plan in store for the both of us, and I'm really thankful he came into my life.

***

I would like to thank Raymari Rodriguez for her blood, sweat, tears, and patience into writing this book. She's learning what the men already knew about me. It takes patience to work with a guy like Thomas. I thank God for bringing her in my life too. I don't look at her as just somebody who works with me, or for me. I look at her as my partner. She's somebody I can go to as well and get advice. She also softens me when I get a little bit too hard, and I need that. I need that sometimes, especially when I am not in a committed relationship in my life. It's good to have a woman who can remind me, to relax. I thank God for her.

***

I thank God for Raymi Rodriguez. He helped me design Team Excel and Subcontracting. It's amazing what God has done. He's put remarkable people in my life. I don't know anything more important in life than your ability to follow an instruction. It's just as equally important whose instructions you follow. I thank God for the members of team Excel; they have put their trust in me with their talents. It's so important to have a group of people of like-mindedness, people who want nothing but the best for you. I am blessed to have found that in all of you.

FORWARD

Is the perfect word to describe Thomas Blandford.
Thomas Blandford is moving ahead and onward and advancing…

Left on the streets of New York City as a teenager, Thomas rises to teach and train youth and adults of today, with similar moorings. Thomas is training others how to overcome the odds and rise to a higher level of achievement. Considering his opposition, it is phenomenal!

Ernest W. Frye
Chairman and Founder
MetroWest Ministries

CHAPTER 1

Life in Shambles

I remember running up the seven flights of stairs as fast as I could trying to get away from some young thug that I knew was trying to hurt me. He was trying to take my money that my aunt gave me, and beat my ass because I wouldn't give it to him.. The building was in shambles, the trash all over the floor, boards and bricks everywhere. A common sight in the seventies in Harlem. At one point, I felt I would never make it. Finally, I arrived at my aunt's apartment door. Trying to get to safety, I started desperately banging on the door to get inside the apartment, and my aunt wouldn't let me in. She peeked out and saw that some-one was following me. But instead of opening the door, she said, "Thomas, You see one of those boards right there? You pick it up and defend yourself." And I did. I sent a kid to the hospital because of an argument that had started over a couple of dollars. At the young age of six, I had my first taste of violence. I would like to say I was scared and that I felt guilty, but the truth is, after seeing what I did to that guy, at that time when I beat him with the board, it felt good. I didn't feel any remorse. I didn't feel any sorrow for what I did. What I did feel was pride, a strange feeling of accomplishment for being able to take care of myself. I felt like a champion. People say some events shape your life. I don't know if that particular event changed me or if it just exposed what I would inevitably turn into.

I finally got inside the apartment, started talking to my aunt, and she engaged me in learning how to box and how to do martial arts. It wasn't long until the family of the kid I had beat up was looking for revenge, so my aunt's friends told me that it was best for me to get out. I moved back in with my family in a town called Elmira. My parents were less than thrilled because I had six sisters and three brothers. I fell somewhere toward the end of that chronology and was the most difficult to handle. My mother and father were married for fifty-eight years. My father, Donald Clayton Blandford, was a military man, not very tall but well toned and very handsome. He had a presence that demanded respect. He was an alcoholic and often abusive toward his children. He would hit us and verbally abuse us when he was drunk. As a child, I did not feel abused. I never looked at him as this terrible parent who did not take care of his children because he was drunk. It doesn't mean he wasn't, but since everyone around our neighborhood lived in the same conditions and most adults in my life were like him or worse, the situation did not faze me. It was our "normal." That's the amazing thing about human minds; we are able to adapt to survive. One interesting thing about my father was that even being an alcoholic, he was also very political. He was president of the local NAACP chapter. He was involved in the Knights of Columbus, the world's largest Catholic fraternal service organization. He belonged to several organizations and clubs. He was very articulate. In fact, at times, he made us read encyclopedias or the dictionary to look things up, which, coming from someone like him, may seem strange. The thing is, movies and TV lead us to believe that people are like the fictional characters we see. They are either the hero or the villain, but humans are way more complex than that, and Donald Blandford was as complex as they get.

My mother, Harriet Ghee Blandford, was the cream of the crop. She was short and fair skinned with jet-black hair. She looked like a movie star and could have been one. She had an effect and class that did not fit with the life-style assigned to her. My mother's family was very poor. My grandmother was white, and my grandfather was black. They both worked the restaurant circuit in the fifties, and in those days, there was a lot of racism, so they were never paid well. They were also alcoholics, and from that was some physical abuse. My mother dropped out of school at age seventeen and married my father. He encouraged her to get her GED and driver's license. The most remarkable part was that even while suffering from multiple sclerosis, she raised ten kids, eight who were hers and two who were grandchildren. As time went on, she even took on the burden of raising two more grandchildren. She practically raised us alone because my father was usually out. She held that house together, or at least she tried.

My house in Elmira was on the east side of town. It was a big house with holes in the roof. When it rained, we had to put old rusted metal buckets on the floor to catch the raindrops coming through the ceiling. My bed was torn, with piss stains and springs coming out of the mattress. We had old wood floors that buckled underneath. The whole house always felt kind of slanted. The black-and-white television with a coat hanger as an antenna served as the only method of entertainment, and it barely worked. My clothes were hand-me-downs, and sometimes, I had to wear my sister's clothes, which were too big. I was made fun of a lot. You know that you are not doing well in life when you live in a bad neighborhood where everyone around you is poor, yet even they look down on you. Apparently, it is human nature to try to feel better about ourselves by putting others down. There were times when we couldn't afford blankets. My mother would share her blankets, and she gave us her coats. We often didn't have heat, and somehow, she managed to keep us alive. She would get us up for school; she would scramble to feed us.

I remember being at school, and at one point, we were asked to draw an animal in a natural setting. I drew a dog standing up on two feet and dressed in a suit and tie with a brim hat on. The dog held a can of Budweiser and smoked a blunt. That was my natural setting. I had created my own "reality," one that I did not want to leave because when I did, the real world smacked me in the face. The dog event served as foretelling to a lot of psychiatrists and psychologists. There was even an incident at one point when I was in a fight in the playground at Ernie Davis Junior High School. The vice principal came over to break up the fight. I picked him up and slammed him on his back. Of course, I was suspended. I just didn't have respect for authority. The teachers didn't really pay much attention to me as I was what you might call a class clown, or they felt like I was just hopeless.

My father was pretty political in those days. Not many people realized how much my father drank and what happened when he did. Plus, back then, you didn't really talk much about what was going on at home. I was often so scared of my dad that I would piss the bed because I did not want to use the bathroom when he came home drunk.. He would wake me up in the middle of the night and the beatings would start. I used to be so afraid of my father, so scared that I didn't even want to go home. Sometimes I would get beat for things I didn't even do. So I would stay out to like three or four in the morning and try to sneak in. I remember one time when all the doors to the house were locked, and all the windows were locked as well, so I took a ladder that was laid up on the side of the house, and I would stand it up on the side of the house so as to be able to climb through the second story window which lead to the bedroom. I got in, turned on light, and to my surprise there was my father. He asked me where I had been and I said out with Dave and them. I guess I must of smelled like alcohol because he said " and you been drinking again too haven't you little nigger!?" I heard that name so much or little devil that I began to think that was my name, or at least my nickname. My father punched me and beat me yet again that early morning. He hit me so hard I was even bleeding from my mouth. It was always an ass kicking or a beat down with him when it came to me. I remember one time when he even threw me up against a burning stove. I guess at that time back then that's just how kids got punished. I forgive my dad now, and I am grateful for the good things that he did try to instill in me and for his many contributions that he willingly made to help better the community. But I am mostly grateful that before he died that I could pray with him and lead him to my savior Jesus Christ! I was about thirteen years old when I finally stopped pissing the bed. Kids would make fun of me because I smelled like piss. Their taunts hurt but also got me stronger and more violent, which of course, got me into more trouble. Teachers, my parents, the law, you name it; I was in trouble with everyone. My father thought it was best to transfer me to a Catholic school, but the new school didn't help because I was such a trouble-maker. At that point in my life, I didn't realize there could be other things, more powerful things than a human being, I didn't think there was a God because if he existed, he had also forgotten about me. He had failed me just like every adult in my life. Deep down, that emptiness bothered me and was one of the reasons I acted out with drugs, violence and alcohol. I couldn't concentrate in Catholic school and always left to go find something or someone more exciting. My father tried to get me help with a psychiatrist and pro-bation people he knew, but that didn't work. I finally got sent back to Ernie Davis Junior High School.

Around the time I was sent back, a group of college students volunteered at the school. They were running a tutoring program for troubled kids. One of the students was Don. Don was a white American guy. He was skinny and had a long, big nose. He was very timid. He was the kind of guy I beat up in school. Don wanted to be a teacher. He asked to work with students who were failing one or more classes, along with the roughest, toughest students, and I had already dropped out of school by then, I was not chosen. I did not care until I found out some of my friends that I hung out with in the alleyway were chosen. I was upset, but mostly, I was jealous. To hide my feelings, I started making fun of those guys, and I was beating them up every time they went to do schoolwork with Don instead of hanging out with me. Don heard about what I was doing and said he wanted to meet me. One day, he pulled up with my friends in a van from the Salvation Army. This skinny white boy was coming into the alleyway, my alleyway, and he would destroy our gang, pull us apart.

He got out and had the nerve to confront me. He said, "If you don't want to go, if you don't want to be of help, that's fine, but these guys want help, and they need help at school. If you don't want to do that, that's fine with me."

I was going to kick his ass. He was not a fighter, and I got so upset at him that I broke the van mirror. I threw rocks at the van and told him to get the hell out of my face.

I guess he felt like I was a project for him to work on, and he found out through other friends that I could dance. So he put on a dance contest and invited me up to come to this dance contest. I said I'm not going to no fucking queer dance contest with all these people judging me.

He knew how to push my buttons though, because he said, "What, are you a punk? Are you scared? Afraid?" I took that challenge and was very upset when I did not come in first place. He was supposed to be responsible for bringing me home, and I never let him take me home. I went drinking and driving with some friends. He tried to get me in the van.

I said, "Fuck you, I'm not going."

He went and told my parents, and of course, my dad beat the hell out of me. The next day, I went to visit Don. I apologized, and he invited me to hang out with him. I did, and we listened to records, and we talked. He started inviting me out and asking if I wanted to go for pizza and stuff like that. He was a Christian and tried to help me, but I just wouldn't listen to him. I loved his friendship though, because it was a different type of friendship. It was something I wasn't used to. Through his actions, he showed he loved me unconditionally. At that stage in my life, Don was the only escape I had from my reality. Unfortunately, it wouldn't last long. Don moved to Massachusetts and left me alone. His departure proved once again to me that nobody cared about me.

One day I was in school and got into an argument with my shop teacher, Mr. Carr. He told me to go to the principal's office. I said, "Fuck this school," and I just walked right out the front door and kept going. A man saw me walking. He asked if I wanted to go to his place and smoke and eat, so I said, "Hell yea!"

Little did I know he had other plans. He came out of his room naked and tried to get me to touch him. I just ran. I was so afraid that I left my coat behind. I saw that man again that night at a party. He asked me what happened. Why did I leave and not come back? I said my dad was waiting for me and he wasn't going to let me back out.

He said, "You're out now."

I said, "Yea, I snuck out while he was drunk, but I got to go with my boys."

I was scared because even though I was living a life of danger with questionable people, alcohol and drugs, the fear on my mind was not only what that man wanted to do to me but also being tormented by people again. I never told anybody for fear I would be labeled a faggot.

At the age of six, I had my first taste of alcohol. By the time I turned nine, I realized that I actually enjoyed it. I would drink beers and steal them from wherever I could. As I got older, I moved on to harder liquor, and even though I continued to enjoy it, it didn't seem to fill the void. At the tender age of twelve, I moved on to drugs. First, it was weed, and then I began to drink and get high at the same time. This is called cross fading and gave me a new kind of high. While I was high, I felt like my problems would go away. I fit in wherever I was. When you share a joint, nobody judges you. Everyone is trying to scrape away their own evil.

I quickly realized that marijuana was just a gateway to other drugs. Once I was around people who smoked weed, it wasn't long until I was exposed to stronger drugs and had the ability to get them. I was probably about fifteen when I tried crack. One day, this girl that I was attracted to went into this building that looked abandoned. She said she would be right out. Well, she took too long to come back out, so I went up to the door and banged on it. People let me in, and there she was sitting on a couch with some girl and another guy. She held this pipe up to my mouth.

Honestly, I really didn't know what it was. I thought it was weed. Shows how even though I felt like I was ahead of my age, street smart and the like, I was just a naive dumb kid. I smoked it. I thought it was the best feeling in the world; I was in a different dimension, a completely different feeling than weed gave me. However, a few minutes later, I found myself getting scared. I could see things that were not supposed to be there, had hallucinations, so I panicked and bolted toward the door, never to go back again.

Once my body got used to the weed, I was searching for something that would give me a stronger high. I began to try anything I could get my hands on: cocaine, speed, whatever. I didn't just try them; I lived just waiting for the next hit, which became my lifestyle. That is who I was.

CHAPTER 2

Self-Destruction

A lot of the older drug dealers gave me the opportunity to be what I looked at as a boss/king. To work for them, run for them and eventually own a business alongside them.

A lot of girls were attracted to Thomas. I had older men who were my street mentors, and they taught me how to get what I wanted from these girls. They taught me how to use these girls, how to make money off of these girls. I was always making money and getting the girls from Elmira to down south to Michigan and Kansas and back. They would travel to make money with the promises of lies and pretending to only love them, promises of gold and silver jewelry, and a great life. They just did whatever the fuck I told them. These girls were young and naïve, and had problems at home as well. And they really were in love with me. So I did what I was taught and took full advantage of it. I made them feel special with bullshit coming out of my mouth. I had a certain look with my eyes that they loved. I would tilt my head slightly to the left side, and roll my eyes up at them. And they felt bad for me, and thought it was so cute they would just leave. Those girls loved them some Thomas. It was so easy to sleep with some of my friends' girls and even my brother's ex-girlfriend. I thought I was the shit! I made girls sell their bodies for me so I could be high or drunk. I even watched while other friends of mine had sex with some so-called girlfriends of mine.

I was selling girls. Making them fall in love with me, giving me drugs, giving me alcohol, having sex with me, having sex with my friends, and I made them do whatever I wanted them to do and promised them the world. A lot of it was because of my height, and I knew how to talk. I had a very good "game."

I was caught once for possession, and the judge was deciding between putting me in jail and letting me go free. He said, "Mr. Blandford, these police officers tend to think because of how short and cute you are that you get away with a lot." The funny thing about it was the judge let me go. Maybe if he hadn't, I might have been better off sooner in life. But he let me go. I don't really know why some people get away with a lot and others don't. Why someone makes one mistake and gets life in prison while others continue to commit crimes and get away with them. What I do know is that sometimes in court, you run into some judges or lawyers, and they want to see the light in you and give you another chance. The problem is there is no follow up, no support for the kids being released into the same surroundings that made them get in trouble in the first place.

I was about 18 years old. I remember hanging out with Dave, a friend of mine. We went to an after-hours party, and the usual crowd was there. We got drunk, and we got high. I met a girl, and she was older than me. She wanted me to go with her to her apartment where she and her cousin were staying. I took Dave with me so he could be with the cousin. We drank and smoked some more. The cousin came out of her room. She had nothing on but a T-shirt. She was prettier than the girl I was with, so I made a move. The first girl noticed my interest, got upset, and told her cousin to put some clothes on. I pretended like I was going to the bathroom and caught the cousin in the hallway. We started making out and moved to the kitchen table. My friend Dave walked toward us and was upset that I was with "his" girl. It's amazing how reality changes when you are under the influence of drugs and alcohol. Here we are in an apartment with girls we have known for less than an hour, yet in our minds we already owned them. There is no conscience telling you that your thoughts don't make any sense. It is just this egotistical psycho directing your body.

Dave was a lot bigger and older than I was. He played football, and he could lift more than two hundred pounds over his head. He grabbed me and picked me off my feet so high up that they dangled in the air. The only thing going through my mind was to get him the fuck off me so I could get back to fucking his girl and mine.

Being so small compared with him, I knew that trying to fight him would be useless, so I looked around, and I saw a big fat butcher knife on the table. I grabbed the knife, and I cut him on his arms and across his chest. Disbelief registered on his face, and he dropped me. He ran out the door screaming and bleeding. I was very scared, petrified.

He lost a lot of blood. I could see the path of blood over several feet of snow. I kept thinking, *Why is the blood so thick?*

Dave passed out around the corner. Within five minutes of me getting there, I was surrounded by police officers. They wanted to arrest me for attempted murder. You've never seen a kid so scared. Yet on the outside, I showed something completely different. I wanted them to see that I really didn't care about life. I was so high and drunk I felt like I was Superman, and as they took me away, I yelled to the paramedics, "Fuck him. Let him die!"

As the time to see the judge drew closer and the alcohol started leaving my body, I began to worry. I wasn't concerned about Dave. I was just thinking about what would become of me. That tough guy wound up being very much a small, little baby.

My father and brother showed up for court. I don't think they were there to support me. They appeared more out of curiosity to see what would become of me.

I felt like my public defender did not do his job. I spoke up, told the judge that this guy Dave was a lot bigger than me. He lifted weights, and I was afraid for my life. I was defending myself, and I felt like the judge was starting to fall for it. Then he asked me a question—a very poignant question. He said, "Let me ask you, Mr. Blandford, what would you have done if there had been a gun on the table?"

Now I could've lied, but I was so proud and had such a stupid attitude, my response was, "I would have shot him."

The judge looked at me with a look of astonishment and then anger. "With that, you are to spend two years in upstate New York in the prison facility," he said.

I actually thought I was going to do life. Then something stupid came out of my mouth again. "Two years is nothing. I'll do that standing on my head."

So the judge responded, "Here's six more months to get you back on your feet."

I did two and a half years for assault and battery with a deadly weapon. I remember hearing the bars close behind me. I remember big, big guys, grown men—I'm a young teenager—coming up to my bunk, threatening me, making all kinds of comments. I remember fighting for my life in there. But I just dealt with situations as they arose. I just didn't care nor did I have any remorse. I wasn't even scared while I was locked up. Just upset that I wasn't getting out when I wanted to. I was the type of guy who loved to be in control and loved freedom. But that was taken from me, and I blamed everybody else. I also felt that as long as I had "my bitches," girls to bring me money, I would be okay. I loved having control over females and having them be conned into selling their bodies for me. To me that was love, and if they didn't do it, then forget them. I would get another girl to take care of me. So that's how I got my comfort, knowing that they would come to see me and bring me money. That was their job.

Most of the girls I dated were solely for my own purposes, but there was a very special lady I was crazy for. Rhonda Ladue was Indian and French, but when I went to jail, she couldn't take seeing me behind bars. She went to visit me, and I had no idea that would be the last time I would ever see her again. I wrote several letters, and she never replied. For the first time in my life, I knew what love was, but was hurt by it.

When I was released, my mother was lying in the bedroom from multiple sclerosis complications. My father had said he was going to work and I needed to go to school. I hated school.

After he left, I decided to throw a party. I invited all of my friends, girls and guys. We stole a keg of beer. We rolled up some joints, took out bags of coke and did our thing. My father came back about a half an hour later. He never went to work. He stayed around the corner. He knew what I was doing and planned to catch me.

When he came back, we were in shock. He picked up every single one of my friends and threw them out of the house. I sat on the couch, scared to death, and he said, "You're next, little nigger."

He picked me up and threw me out. This was in the winter, and there was snow on the ground. I was screaming for my life, for my mother to come and help me even after I totally disrespected her when she was on her deathbed. She couldn't help me. She was stricken, bedridden. It was cold, and I didn't have any clothes but the clothes on my back, and I was barefoot. I was scared to death. I tried to stay at other friends' houses, and their parents wouldn't let me. So for the first time in my life, I think that I was actually really scared. I did not know where to go. All my "buddies" who had opened their doors to me when I wanted to buy drugs or sell girls now turned their backs on me. A friend gave me an old coat and a pair of old sneakers two sizes too big. He allowed me to sleep on his back porch with nothing to cover up with other than the coat. When I woke up the next day, I called Don in Massachusetts. He said I could stay with him but had to get there on my own. So I hitch-hiked out to Massachusetts.

CHAPTER 3

Wandering

On the way to Massachusetts, I ran into a lot of different characters, a lot of different people. There are people who have a protective instinct when they see someone in need, and there are people who see an opportunity to take advantage of the weak. The latter seemed to be the most common among people who picked up hitchhikers. I ran into men who looked like respectable businessmen, only to find out they wanted me to pay them with sexual favors. When I refused, they threw me out.

I remember a couple stopping to give me a ride. I felt comfortable with them. They were laid back and friendly. They drank alcohol and had no problem sharing. They started smoking weed, and they were into other drugs as well. At that point, I felt like I had hit the jackpot. We were on the road for a while. The man smoked a joint a certain way; it's called a shotgun. He gave this joint to his wife and told her to give me a shotgun. It's basically where you blow the smoke in the opposite direction, and the person inhales the smoke. She did, and she was trying to kiss me at the same time. I felt uncomfortable not because I had an issue with kissing the man's wife, but because I didn't want to lose my ride and the free drugs.

He said to go ahead, and then he told me to reach down her shirt. When I reached down her shirt, he started cursing at me and said, "What the hell you think you're doing?"

I said, "You told me to do it."

He said, "I'm going to fucking pull over, and I'm going to kill you."

I jumped out before he even stopped the car. I rolled, and I just kept running. I ran through the woods. I had this big old coat on, no other clothes, and I just was scared to death. I hid behind a tree, and I just shook. My shoes had fallen off. I stayed there for what seemed like hours in the freezing cold, when I felt like it was safe, I went back and got my shoes. I returned to the highway to start hitchhiking again.

Finally, I convinced Don to meet me in Albany, New York, at the turnpike. He drove me to his place in Massachusetts and I agreed to get a job and start making money to get my own place. The plan that he and I came up with was for me to move out into my own place once I saved up enough money. When I finished collecting money with the kettles for an organization, I had earned enough money to get my own place. But I wanted to go back to Elmira for Christmas. Don gave me an ultimatum that if I went back home and I spent all my money, that I could not come back to live with him. I said that I was not going to spend all my money. However, I went home and I blew all my money. I was trying to be a show off so I spent money on booze, drugs, my friends and girls. I wanted to be the hot shit of Elmira. Sometimes what you really think you are to yourself or to others, you're really not, and you're only fooling just yourself (be true to yourself always). When I got there, things seemed to be a little better. He had some conditions and some rules. He said there would be no drinking and no drugs. I would have to go back to school, and I agreed. I had a dream of living in a peaceful home with someone who cared about me. I wouldn't have to be scared of my drunken father coming for me at night. It was a blank slate, and I could be whoever I wanted to be. I tried. I gave it my best effort, but it wasn't long until I found people who did what I did.

I started drinking and doing drugs again. I found a girl, and I stayed with her and her family so that I could party. At two, three o'clock in the morning, the mother got upset and threw me out. Don would not let me in. I climbed up the drainpipe, and I broke into his apartment. He said, "You can stay the night. But tomorrow you're going to a shelter. If you come and you break in again, I'm calling the police."

The next day he dropped me off at this shelter. I slept between two folding metal chairs. There was one guy on the left, one guy on the right. One guy was shitting his pants, and the other guy was leaning over, throwing up, puking on the floor. Here I am in the middle of both of them. I was scared to death. There were a lot of people—a lot of men. I was so scared that I couldn't sleep. I didn't dare sleep. I didn't take off my shoes. I didn't do anything but just lay between those chairs just holding myself, wondering what would happen to me.

When I got up the next day, they said you had a certain time you had to be back. If you're not, you lose your spot. I didn't go back. I started sleeping outside. I started staying with girls. I stayed with other friends, and basically, I wound up in jail. Don, again, came back and helped me. Told me I could stay, but if I messed up again he was taking me back to New York.

Guess what? I messed up again. I got a job working for the Salvation Army, ringing bells for the kettles for Christmas, and that did not fit me. I had to wear the hat, I don't wear hats, and I don't like hats. That was my mentality. I did the work for a little bit, thinking I could steal money during lunch break. With the money, I got somebody to buy me a bottle of whiskey. I took that bottle of whiskey; I hid it in my pocket. When Don came to pick me up, he dropped me off at his apartment. He had to work. I went inside his apartment and started drinking the whiskey.

He was coming back. I could hear him coming up the stairs, and of course, my heart was pounding because I was about to lose this place. I hid the bottle of whiskey underneath the cushion of the couch. Where he stayed, there was a gym so I would go down to the gym, and I would play basketball, run around, chase girls, whatever, and he'd be up in the apartment. Somehow he found that bottle of whiskey.

He said, "Thomas, I want to talk to you. You need to leave. You need to go now. I don't need you to come back.

You obviously cannot respect my rules. You obviously do not understand that I'm doing you a favor."

I was scared again. I started crying, and I said, "No. Please don't throw me out. I have nowhere to go."

He said, "I don't care. You need to leave."

I left, and I was on the streets all over again, by myself, in the winter with no place to go. Most of the time, I just stayed awake getting high and getting drunk with other people. Finally, I hitchhiked back to New York. I stayed with friends, got high, got drunk. I just did not care. I did cocaine. I just did any drug that was out there. I would try to get back into my parents' house, and my father would give me a chance, but I'd turn around and do the same old thing again. Robbing, stealing, drinking, drugging, bringing girls in when he was at work and stuff, and finally, my dad just said, "It's over. You just can't."

Same thing with my friends: "You just can't stay here no more. You're just not getting this."

A year later, Don had moved to his father's house. I asked if I could come back. I promised him that I'd changed. He lived with his parents and talked to them. He called me back and said I could stay with them for a while.

I didn't change. I went there. I stayed, and I would come in late at night and I'd be drunk, and I'd be high.

Not a week had gone by when Don's father said, "Your friend Thomas doesn't respect the rules."

At this point, I was a little older so I felt like I was boss. Like I was king. I told myself I didn't care and that it didn't bother me. At that point I felt like nobody loved me anyway. I felt like sex was love. I felt like as long as I had girls doing what I wanted them to do, I could get high. I could get drunk. I didn't care.

That lasted for a little while. Some of these girls got smart very quick. When you've got girls that you tell you love and then you've got your friends laying with those girls, and they're paying you to do that, it gets old fast.

So I was back out in the streets of Framingham, Massachusetts. I was running around, and I had this moment where I really just thought: "It's time to change. It's really time to grow up."

So I called Don again. He said, "No, you can't stay here. But my mom will let you stay outside in the backyard of the house in a tent."

It was wintertime. Something about me being homeless in the wintertime. I set up a tent in the backyard.

Don said, "Listen, you need to get a job, and you need to get one now. I'll help you. I'll come and pick you up, and I'll help you get your education."

That was stupid because I hated it. I hated school. We just didn't get along. At first I got a job working at Wendy's at Natick/Framingham Line. Don would pick me up, and he'd try to help me get my GED. That didn't work out so well. I kept coming back to the tent. I felt like that was home for me. Because I felt like I had a tent, I had a sleeping bag, I could get high, I could get drunk, and nobody could tell me what to do. I was my own boss.

Eventually this guy, he had a certain ministry, and he worked with young men in the ministry at the Salvation Army. I was at the Salvation Army with him and we were listening to this activist by the name of Jesse Jackson, and he was giving a speech at the Democratic Convention. He had talked about covering up with patches that his mother had sewn together to make a blanket and how poor they were. Here was Jesse Jackson now, once a presidential candidate, now speaking at the Democratic Convention. So when I heard this man speak, I connected with him. I turned around, and I looked at my friend.

I said, "I want to get my GED. But I have nowhere to stay that's warm and everything. I really do want to get my GED."

So he talked to the pastor of the Salvation Army. They let me stay there. I swore up and down I wouldn't drink, I wouldn't bring any girls, and I would not do anything to upset them. They made an exception for me because nobody was supposed to be living there. At night when everybody left, I'd get somebody to buy me liquor or booze, and at one point, I brought in a bag of cocaine. I did not know that I left a trail of it on the floor.

I went up into the room where I was staying, and the pastor got me up early in the morning. He found the trail of cocaine on the floor, and he knew it was mine. In my room, he found a bottle of wine. He found some beer bottles, some girly magazines. I was just totally disrespectful to the church and to the Salvation Army. He sat me down in his office, and he told me that I had to leave. I started to cry because it really hurt, and I felt like it was unfair that I got kicked out again. My father had kicked me out. My friends had kicked me out. Now the church was kicking me out. When he told me to leave and I told him I had nowhere else to go, and he said that was not his problem, I turned around, and I insulted him and swore at him.

I was able to convince Don's mom to let me stay in the tent again. I kept my job at Wendy's, but I had had no way of getting there. It was a distance. So Don told me that he would pick me up. He'd give me a ride to work. He'd take me to school, but he came up with an idea. The idea was for me to save my money to buy a bike so I could get back and forth to work. Now the other part of that was I would have no money to get high anymore or to get drunk anymore. So I had to make a choice. But I liked the idea of having my own bike, so I said okay. I would give him some money. I would lie about how much I made. He was a teacher, and eventually he knew I was lying, and he wanted to see the pay stubs. He started taking all the money.

I remember one point when I was in the GED class that Don taught and I just couldn't grasp school. I couldn't grasp this stuff. At one point, I threw a chair at him and I told him. I said fuck you, fuck school, fuck the whole damn thing! I didn't care. I just hated it, and I got very angry; and a lot of times, when I get angry, I blank out. I just go off and I went off. I tore up the school and he kicked me out of there. He ignored me for quite a while and I had to beg for his forgiveness, beg for him to take me back, and finally he did, probably about two weeks later. I went back, I studied, I drank, and I got high still and I had women still. But I studied hard with him, and I worked. I used that money to save for a bike, and I got a bike. Getting that bike was the first accomplishment I ever made in my life. I had a friend of mine who was the manager at Wendy's. His name was Paul.

He said to me, "You get your high school diploma, and I'll let you become a manager here."

Time went on. I got my high school diploma, and Don said to me, "You don't have to be a manager. You can go on further. You can go to college now. You can do anything you want. You don't have to be a manager at Wendy's."

So with that being said, I quit my job at Wendy's, and I started another job in the loading dock of the Salvation Army. I wanted to be close to church. I wanted to be close to God. I wanted to get my life right. I got me another room, and I started working at the loading dock of the Salvation Army, making less money there than I was at Wendy's. But I felt like at that point I was going to change my life.

CHAPTER 4

A Bottle and a Bride

I basically started hanging out with a gentleman who was an alcoholic and drug addict. But he had an apartment, and he had a girlfriend who was friends with a girl called Denise. From what I heard, Denise was attracted to my butt, and I actually flirted with her a little bit. They invited me up to the apartment.

We started drinking, smoking some joints, doing some blow, and talking dirty, playing cards. Denise was dating another guy. My attitude was I could take her from him, and I did. My thinking was that I just wanted to have sex with her. I didn't really love anybody. I just didn't know what love was. So all I really wanted was to have sex with her, and it was just another quest for me. I went outside, and I talked to her, and she had two children.

I fed her a line of bull, "I guess it comes as a package deal." Want to know the truth? The truth is I did not care about those kids.

She thought I was good looking. We kissed, went inside, and I tried to have sex with her that night. She was sleeping on the couch and wouldn't have sex with me.

I slept on the floor and thought, "I'm going to have sex with this woman." Now I damn sure don't believe in taking it. All right? But I do damn sure believe in working for it. So when she said she would not have sex with me, I made a plan. And the plan was all I've got to do with that woman is marry her and I'll have sex with her. Now that was my thinking process. Under the influence of drugs and alcohol, I decided that would be a perfect solution.

With that in mind, I used my skills to convince her. We ended up living in North Reading with her grand-mother. I had no place to go. So my typical belief was to use women to get what I wanted. Eventually, we moved into a condominium complex, paid for by her. I promised her I was going to provide for her and marry her, we had sex and nothing changed. We would fight a lot and argue a lot, and I would party a lot. Sometimes the kids would see that, and back then, I really didn't care. I guess my plan was to just have a wedding. I had a friend I hung out with in that condominium complex, and he said something that I liked. He said, "It's another reason to party, man." I agreed with him. Marriage was just another reason to have a party.

So I went out and bought a ring, and had the wedding right in the house. Her kids were there and so was her fam-ily, I didn't bother telling mine about it. The justice of the peace came to the house to marry us. Denise was pregnant with my baby at that point and right there with a bottle in my hand and a blunt in the other we did our vows. We of course had a party afterward. That same night I went out with my friend, and we stayed out until four-thirty in the morning. When I got home, Denise and I got in another fight. We fought a lot. Our relationship was never steady among the drugs, alcohol and my attitude. We were always fighting. We would often break up, but for some reason, I would always get back together with her.

She definitely had a hard time with me. I met some people in her family and friends of hers, and I made out with her sisters and her friends. At one point, I even got into bed with her mother. I was able to talk my way back with Denise. One reason is she had some kids, and I used them for my leverage. I would always say, "I'm sorry. I'll never let it happen again," and things like that.

She threw me out a lot, and eventually we got to a point where I got very physical. I never hit her, but I would punch the walls, throw things around, and call her names. The kids were crying. Cops were called, and I would go to jail again. But she would always take me back.

One night, I decided to go out to drink. I ran into a guy who lived in the same condominium complex. He was younger, and I thought he would join me to party. Keep me company, so I offered to buy some alcohol and drugs. I used the children's checks to pay. Sadly, when you have an addiction, you don't think of anyone but yourself. I think it's very important that people understand sometimes that money doesn't go where it really needs to be going—to the children. I got with this man, Blake Neeland, and he said he didn't drink. But he went with me to the store, and I started drinking, and he started talking.

He said he'd like to hang out. He wanted to know what apartment I lived in. I gave him the number, and he said he'd like to talk to me sometime and hang out sometime, but he couldn't then. He had to get up for work. I basically went back to my complex, sat outside and got drunk. That was it. I passed out. The very next day that same guy came to my house. I was hung over. I did not remember promising him to go to Bible study that morning.

My wife said, "Well, you've got to keep your word. You told him you were going."

I know she was desperate. She wanted something to change, and this gave her some hope. I went to Bible study with him, and there I met some of the most caring people I've ever met. They just listened to what I had to talk about. I asked questions about religion. I asked questions about Christianity. I asked questions about God, and they tried to help me the best they could. He took me back home. He walked with me back home. He gave me a hug, and that was it.

I didn't stop partying, but I kept going to this Bible study. Eventually, I made it to the church, and there were hundreds of people. I met so many nice folks. They were just different, and I saw something different in them, and I wanted that.

After the church service was over, a lot of people took my phone number. They said, "We're going to help you get a job. We're going to help you get back in school. Whatever you'd like, we're going to help you get."

About a week later, these two men showed up at my door, and they said, "We're going to help you get a job. You need to take care of your family."

I couldn't believe it. They did, and I had a job at CVS, and I had a job at Friendly's Restaurant. I was working both jobs, and they would take me to work and pick me up after work. It was amazing. I would go to the studies with them, and I would go to church with them and praise God. They started studying with me about being saved and about being baptized, and I was baptized.

Then it all came crashing down again. I was across the street from where Blake and I lived, and I was in a pizza joint playing some video games and stuff. He came in and said, "There's something I've got to tell you." He said, "I'm leaving and then I said to myself great! My father kicked me out. My friends kicked me out. The church has kicked me out."

Now he was leaving. He was like my brother.

"I'm going to Florida," he said.

Of course there was a lot of words exchanged, a lot of cursing, a lot of yelling, a lot of crying. I wasn't going to go back home to my wife Denise at the time. I decided I was going to go back to the streets to party some more, where I didn't feel rejected. Blake and a couple of the guys came and found me, and they put me in a house with single Christian men, way out of the way. A place so isolated that, if you don't have a car, you are not going anywhere. They got me up at four o'clock in the morning to spend time with God. We went out on a walk. We'd walk in the morning, and we'd read our Bibles, and we'd pray. They'd have quiet time outside at night to spend time with God. Then you got home, you got dressed, and you went to work. They took me to work, and when I didn't want to get up, they would flip the bed upside down on me and say, "You're getting up."

These were guys who went to Boston College, Harvard University. These were football and basketball players, guys who were born-again Christians, and they were not a joke. They loved God, and they meant sincerely to help people change their lives. I did want to go back to my wife, and they said, "You're going to go back after we talk to your wife."

They talked to my wife, and there was a gentleman by the name of Gordon Ferguson who was one of the elders and leaders of the church. He counseled my wife and me. At first my wife did not want anything to do with me. She was with some other people from another church, and eventually they were able to convince her to at least sit down and talk so we could try to reconcile what we had left of a marriage. I'll never forget that I was really disruptive with Gordon when he was trying to talk to my wife, and the man just blurted out, "Shut up."

Nobody ever talked to me like that without getting hurt. Nobody did. But I did. I shut up, and I listened. After that counseling session, Denise and I went back home.

We eventually hated where we were living in Reading, Massachusetts, so we decided to move to Framingham. We thought it would be a fresh start. Unfortunately, it wasn't. In Framingham, we moved to a duplex, and I didn't change. Her sister came up to visit; again, I made a pass with her sister. Her sister eventually left. I still did a lot of drinking, partying, yelling, screaming and fighting. I went back to all of that.

I thought another reason to party was to have another wedding. I thought, *This time it's going to be better.* It's going to be different so I want to rededicate my vows. We do it right with the church this time.

So we did it this way, and I was sober. We went to church, we got married, and I had a party afterward in the backyard. That did not make a difference.

CHAPTER 5

A Dark Hole

Blake was gone. There was no way to get help for me. I didn't care about the church. I didn't care about God. I didn't care about the kids. I just didn't care, and I ran around with other women. Having people like Blake come into my life and then leave caused more harm than good because it felt like they would raise me higher to let me fall, and each time it hurt more.

I got to a very low point. I felt so alone and was drowning in my own desperation. I guess the reason I thought things would change is because I would have some talks with some good friends who loved me and cared about me. At that moment while in the conversation, I felt that my life was about to change, but no matter how much someone wants something for you, it can't happen until you want that for yourself. What would happen is some type of argument would flare up between Denise and me, and I'd go right back to it.

My addictions kept pulling me in, kept telling me they were my only escape. The voices in my head were the voices of addiction. They said, "She doesn't get you, your friends don't get you, and nobody understands you."

It got so bad to the point where I felt like I couldn't get out of it. I felt drowned in my problems and the troubles I was having.

I had a police officer escort me out of my home because I had a restraining order. I saw the police car driving away, and I was already heading back to the house. When I got there, nobody was home. Both the doors and windows were locked, but that did not stop me. In broad daylight, I broke the window to the front door, and I broke into the house. I was so intoxicated I passed out on the floor. Denise found me there and called the police. I got thrown out again and went to another friend's house. I started gambling and drinking. I was basically in my mind going to use Denise because I knew she was in love with me. I made her think that I was in love with her. I was not in love with her. I was incapable of loving anyone because I was always drunk or high, and I was very much incapable of loving her or any-one. I don't even think I loved the kids. I had not worked, I had lost my job, and I basically was hustling stuff. I was selling stuff out of the house to continue my habits.

If my father had taught me anything, it was to be involved in the community. He taught me that it was important to have respect and be part of the political scene. While I was in Framingham, I got involved with politics. I knew how to fake it, and my plan was to have people on my side. Even if I got in trouble with the law, I would have judges and police officers on my side. To some extent, my plan worked. I went to court to contest the restraining order Denise had against me. I shaved, got my haircut low, and I dressed up. I went looking like a lawyer. I gave a wink to the judge, told him I learned my lesson and would get help for the alcohol. He let me go. Against Denise's wishes, he dropped the restraining order. I went back home, and I went right back to drinking.

I was not making any money, I was not providing for my children and didn't want a job. I was not proactive, and all I felt like doing was gambling, getting high and drunk. Denise was desperate. She was suffering. One afternoon, we were at the dinner table. The kids were eating and doing what six-year-olds and eight-year-olds do. I was drunk and getting annoyed. I noticed my daughter's elbow on the table, and I got so upset I banged her arm with my elbow. Denise was very upset, but it didn't faze me because at the time I was intoxicated and felt that I was doing the right thing by sending a message to the other kids that I was the boss.

Denise threatened to call the police again and get another restraining order. I thought I would teach her a lesson. I waited until the kids were at school. She was out of the house, and I was afraid she was with some other guy. So I devised a plan on how to get the attention I wanted from her. I needed to make her feel guilty. I waited until right before she was coming home and before the kids were coming home. I tied a rope around a hook and the other end around my neck.

Denise called Don to take me away. She did get yet another restraining order. I came back very upset about that fact that my plan did not work. I got into an argument, got loud, and the cops arrested me because I broke the restraining order. I went to jail. For court, I wore a tie, and my clothes were clean and pressed. I was very scared because this time I thought I was going to jail. I had a very long record.

However, I carried myself with confidence and planned to get sympathy from the court. I told my lawyer that I had a drinking and drug problem and that I needed help. The court made an offer. I could go to rehabilitation or do the jail time. Although to most people, it would be a clear choice, I was not able to make that decision right away. I told the court I would like to have time to think about it because I'd like to get input from people I trust who are trying to help me. The court allowed me a week. I was shocked to be released. I promised for that week to not touch any drugs or any alcohol.

CHAPTER 6

Another Wasted Chance

I got input and advice from friends. They felt that I needed rehabilitation because they knew if I went to jail, I would come back out, and I would just be the same old Thomas. But that's not the argument they gave me because they knew that wouldn't work. The argument they used was that in a rehab center, you're allowed more freedom. They said the rehabilitation center would be like a paid vacation. Everything would be done for me and so forth. I was convinced, and again I felt like I had outsmarted the system. I got to go somewhere, do whatever I wanted, and they would feed me and give me a place to stay. I called my lawyer and told him I would take rehabilitation at Dick Van Dyke Rehabilitation Center. So he informed the court, I went to court, and I signed the papers agreeing to rehab.

I packed my bag; I could not take any mouthwash, toothpaste or deodorant. I could not take anything that contained alcohol. I said good-bye to my kids and said good-bye to my wife. Don drove me to the rehabilitation center, and as I said good-bye to him, I started to realize rehab would probably be just like jail as far as I was concerned. I could not make phone calls and could not have any contact whatsoever with the outside world. The difference was I probably would've had access to some sort of drugs and alcohol in jail unlike rehab. The more I learned about what they expected from me, the angrier I grew. I was angry because I felt like I was tricked. When I got there, I found out I could not have contact with anybody for six months—not until the last two weeks.

The first month is a drying-out period. You are allowed a little more freedom, but after that, they got very strict. You had to get up at a certain time for breakfast, you had to get up at a certain time for lunch, and you had to get up at a certain time for dinner. You had to make your bed. You couldn't go off the grounds. There were a lot of rules and discipline, which was really lacking in my life. I didn't mind the structure; it felt comforting not to think about what I had to do next. I understand it wasn't just about the alcohol. I had to go to a lot of meetings, three or four meetings a day. No television. Everything was focused on you getting sober.

The meetings made me think more about doing drugs and alcohol. I said to myself I was going to beat this and I was going to get the hell out of here. I wouldn't have to worry about courts anymore, I wouldn't have to worry about judges anymore, and I wouldn't have to worry about getting arrested anymore.

In the back of my mind, I was always contemplating. So I said in the back of my mind, "I'll beat this shit and then I'll get out of here, and I won't even have to worry about probation."

However, I did know there was one catch. If I got in trouble again, I would go straight to jail. I would do about three and a half years in prison. When I was at Dick Van Dyke, all I could think about was what to do when I got out. How I was going to have a big party, who I would see, who I would hang out with, what bars I would hit, smoking a big fat blunt. Rehab did not seem to be working.

I did the six months, and the very last day, I got a letter. I noticed that the letter had arrived two weeks before, and I felt that the counselor kept that letter from me on purpose to test me.

I was packing, I was getting ready to leave, and I said, "Why the fuck did you give me this now? Why didn't you give it to me sooner?" I went off about the place and how I felt about the whole experience.

The counselor actually had the power to make you stay there longer if you were not cooperative, and he said, "Do you want to stay another six months?"

I said, "I don't give a fuck if I stay here my lifetime." I continued to swear at him and told him he could throw me in jail if he wanted to.

I said, "I shouldn't have listened to my friends. The only reason why I'm here is because my friends talked me into coming here. I didn't give a shit."

I went to my room, closed the door, and he waited about an hour before I could even leave. He said, "You're going to be the last one to leave. You have about an hour. Calm down."

I said, "I'm not leaving. I don't give a shit." They could come and arrest me. I closed my door to my room and locked the door. He had the keys and came in about an hour later.

He said, "Listen, I want to talk to you."

He believed I had great potential and told me to get a job! That I could make it out there. The staff talked to me about getting on medication called Antabuse. I agreed, keeping silent about the fact that medication always had a reverse effect on me. I listened and signed a release contract.

Of course, when I got home there was a celebration. I went out, I got high, and I got drunk. I did not follow any of the instructions for aftercare. I was free, and that was how I felt.

CHAPTER 7

The Proposition

Rehab had been a waste of time. A few months later, I did not have a job, my wife was ready to divorce me, and my self-destructive behavior continued to get worse. I was getting home at two and three o'clock in the morning, getting high, getting drunk, and soon I was not going to have a place to stay again.

My friends didn't want me; they couldn't let me stay with them because of what I was doing. Drowned in the feeling of loneliness again and feeling like nobody cared about me, I said forget them all. I'll just end it now. That way nobody has to worry about me anymore. I went to the store, bought a fifth of vodka, went out on the front porch, and took a big fat butcher knife. Said, "I'm going to drink this, I'm going to take some pills, I'm going to smoke my last joint and then I'm cutting my throat." I drank that vodka, took the pills, and smoked my joint. I was starting to cut myself when suddenly this kid named Glenn whom

I used to party with came by and said he had to talk to me. He had a business he wanted to talk to me about.

I noticed he had a brand-new car, so of course, I thought it was drugs. "All right, let's go for a ride," I said.

He said that we would not go for a ride nor would we drink. He told me to clean up and wash my face. We would go for a walk. It was the middle of winter, and he wanted me to be alert for what he had to say. He told me about a marketing business and how he thought I had the perfect personality for it.

I felt encouraged that someone saw something in me. Maybe I wanted him to think I was more together than I really was, but I decided to mention that I was thinking about taking some college courses. Thinking maybe he would be impressed. However, his face didn't change. He asked me some very poignant questions about business. He also asked me how much I thought professors in college made.

I said, "I don't know. Maybe $50,000."

He said, "Is that the kind of money you want to really make?"

I said no. He said, "What do you want to make?"

I said about $100,000 or more.

"Then why are you going to learn from people that make less?"

I thought that he made a good point. He went on to ask, "Do you want to wear the kind of clothes they wear?"

I said no. I wanted to wear Armani suits, and he said, "Well, I'm going to take you to meet some people. Go get dressed."

I told him I didn't have any dress clothes. He said to just clean up. We drove to this house with a long driveway. The house was so big you could drive a car in it. The guy was a doctor, and they were Italian. I thought I'd hit the motherload in selling drugs. I thought I was working for the mob.

When I asked how I could join, the guy smacked me in the back of the head and said, "What's the matter with you?" He said not all Italians are in a mob just like all blacks don't like chicken, and all blacks don't like watermelon.

He explained that what they had was a legitimate, legal business. He said, "Obviously Glenn thought something of you and wants to help save your life. Are you interested?"

"I'm listening," I said.

"I've got some friends who are going to come by," he said. "We're going to talk to you, we're going to talk to your wife, we're going to help put your marriage together, and we're going to talk to you about the business. But you've got to be clean, you've got to be sober, and you've got to be straight."

"Yes, sir, I will be," I said.

I left there excited. I saw what kind of life I wanted to have. I never could relate to having a nine-to-five job, to die poor on Social Security. I always felt like that was very depressing. However, this lifestyle seemed attainable, worth getting clean for. That night, Denise smiled. She could see that I looked different. But by the next day, the urge of drinking defeated me. The men came back two days later and found me drunk and high. They turned around and left.

Months went by. I was still partying, just basically wandering around, and Denise called these people from the business. I was yelling and screaming, and they told me to shut up. They wanted nothing to do with a drunk.

I got in my car, I drove off, and I went on top of this hill. I decided I have got to try to kill myself. I said, "This has got to work. This has got to happen." I wanted to hurt everybody. I was going to drive my car off the top of the hill. I was right at the edge, closed my eyes, and the car swerved back on the road. I believed in God, but I just didn't know about this miracle stuff. I tried three times, and the car kept going back on the road. I couldn't kill myself. I did not know what God had in store for me. So I stayed on the hill and just cried.

I saw this older white guy with a Cadillac. I recognized him because he was in the marketing business. I followed him to his home and found his phone number. The next day, in a drunken stupor I called him up at two-thirty in the morning.

"Sir, you don't know me, but my name is Thomas Blandford," I said. "You'll never have to hear from me again, but it's obvious you are doing well. I need to know how you did it."

"You've got a lot of balls calling me at two o'clock in the morning," he replied. "Do you have a pot of coffee? Put a pot of coffee on. My wife and I will be there at eight-thirty in the morning."

I felt overwhelmed, and I started yelling and screaming because I was so happy I was jumping for joy.

"Wait a minute," he said. "Just one more thing. Don't ever call me at two-thirty in the morning."

He showed up in his Cadillac as promised. His wife wore a fur coat, and he wore a suit and carried a brief-case. This impressed me. My neighbors were sitting out-side. They were drug dealers and criminals, and this couple went and shook their hands. I was sure they were going to get robbed.

In the house, they explained how the marketing busi-ness worked. I felt like it was something right up my alley. I felt like it wasn't an impossible dream. I saw the business opportunity. The man sat there on one side of the dining room table. I sat on the other, and I looked over at Denise. She shook her head from the couch. She didn't want to be part of it. But I had made the decision. I wanted money. I never wanted a boss. He gave me one week to come up with $600.

I started collecting cans, and I begged people for the money. I borrowed the money, I sold my stuff, and at the end of the week, I had the money. Normally I would've spent that money on drugs, alcohol or prostitutes. Not this time. Even though I was still drinking, that money belonged to the business, and the business would change my life. The man came, and I had pennies and nickels and dimes and dollars. He counted every bit of it and gave me a license to start a business with him.

He started training me and spent about three days with me. He got into franchising, and the third day, he said he was moving. I was devastated. It always seemed like people I started getting close to left. I was given the challenge to invite three or four people to my house. He promised he would lead the meeting one last time and then he and his wife were leaving. I was determined to get people there. I asked the drug dealers to come. I went around the corner to the people I used to gamble with and asked them to come. I asked my friends and family to come. I went door to door, talking to people, telling them about this opportunity. People I got high with, people I got drunk with. During the course of conversation with these people, we always talked about having a dream, having our homes, having nice cars and a lot of money.

Sixty people showed up, but the guy was fifteen minutes late. I was getting very nervous, and Denise was getting nervous, so I called him. He told me to do it.

I did the marketing plan with my back facing them. I never turned around. All sixty people signed on board, and I don't even know what I showed them. I have no clue. But all sixty people got in that same night, and we had what we call a registration party. We registered them, and my life had just started turning at that point. I received a check in the mail, and I celebrated by getting drunk and getting high.

CHAPTER 8

A Beer and a Prayer

I was very upset because the check wasn't as much as I thought it would be, so I drank and smoked more. I argued and fought with the man who helped me. Later I understood what was supposed to be happening and how I was supposed to build this thing. I started treating this business like I did selling drugs. I used people, even the women I got in the business. I wanted them to dress a certain way to entice men to come into the business. I flirted with some of the women; even though they knew I was married, I asked them out. My character had not changed. If anything, the money made me show off even more, and I acted like I was a big shot. Since I failed to change my mentality, my failure was inevitable. The bliss lasted a very short term, and eventually Denise asked me for a divorce again.

I went into a deep depression for about a year. I did not shave, I did not shower, and I barely ate. I had people calling me; I would not talk to them. Denise tried to call some people to help me, but I would not talk to anyone.

I kept the blinds to the house closed. Don finally came to the house, and he talked about praying with me. I had a lot of mixed feelings, and I did not want him to pray with me. I actually told him that I was very angry with God because of the drinking, my wife's leaving and my inability to care for the kids.

"I'm no fucking good to anybody," I said. "I'm not doing shit with my life. I let the business go."

He reminded me that I still owned the business. "You can get back on your feet. You can do this."

We talked for about an hour. He'd left work to come see me, and he said, "Maybe I can't pray with you, but I can damn sure pray for you so I'm going to pray for you." And he took off.

I had been involved with a very strict church, and the church had told me I was going to hell. I believed it. Don reminded me that the kingdom of Heaven was within me, and I got on my knees. I cried and started talking to God and praying to God. He said the same exact words. I could hear this faint voice saying, "The kingdom of heaven is within you, Thomas."

So I got up. I cleaned up my act, I went out, and I told Don I needed help getting a job. I needed to put a resume together. Could he help me? I got work as a car salesman. I learned sales techniques there with their materials and their training. Eventually, I got very good at selling. I got into a dispute with one of the managers about selling a car to a lady who had just lost her husband. They wanted me to "take off her head." I refused. I think it was because she reminded me of my mother.

I got another sales job and became the number one salesman for four months in a row. For some reason, I was able to separate my outside problems when I went into my job. I felt like the customers didn't know me, and I could be whomever I chose to be. I was succeeding at work, yet I still had a lot of court problems that I had to clear up. I still partied, I still drank, and I still wanted to kill myself. I was wrestling with something within me. I came home drunk one night, and Denise and I were arguing again. Unexpectedly, my twelve-year-old son jumped into the argument. He was big for his age, and I guess at that point, he was sick of listening to the same argument over and over again. He started yelling and being disrespectful.

Something came over me, and I just took him by the throat and picked him up. I was choking him almost to the point where he couldn't breathe. Denise got me off him. I noticed the other kids saw what I had done. Everyone was screaming, calling me a drunk and a child abuser. I looked at my children's faces, and all I could see was the same fear I had when my father used to come home drunk. It was the worst feeling in the world. I knew I was a drunk and a druggie, but I never wanted to be feared by my own children.

Feeling like the lowest dirt, I went to a nearby bar and got drunk again. I went to a friend's house. I used to gamble with him, and we started drinking heavily. For three days in a row I did not eat. I kept drinking day and night until I would lose consciousness and then I would wake up and do it all over again. We invited girls over, had sex and partied. I had this empty feeling. I was not even enjoying the drugs. Nothing could numb the pain. My brain started to drift into the darkness, and I contemplated committing suicide again. Maybe this time I could actually do it; maybe this would be the time that I would stop the pain and free my family from the monster I was becoming. I sent my friend to get a thirty-rack of beer, and I was left alone.

I looked around, wondering what I would do this time to end it all. For some reason, I decided to call Deryck Frye, pastor of MetroWest Worship Center, the church I attended back then. I said to God before I called the church, "Listen, the only way I'm going to knock this stuff off is if you intervene right now in my life. If somebody— the pastor has to answer this phone or I'm going to go back out, and I'm going to try and kill myself again, and you'll be sorry, and everybody else will be sorry."

I was pushing my luck. Who is going to answer the phone at nine o'clock at night in an office? But somebody did. The secretary stated that Pastor Deryck Frye was not in, but Pastor Ernie Frye was in, and he was getting ready to take a trip to Dominican Republic. I told her I was going to kill myself. So she got the pastor right away.

He had maybe half an hour before he had to leave to catch the flight. We started talking. I told him about my life, how my father was abusive toward me. All the drinking and drugging, the cheating and growing up on white people economy. Being a "nigga" and black people, my life, how we lived. The drinking, the partying. I spilled it all out from how I used women, how I prostituted women and how I tried to kill myself before.

He said something that actually caught my attention. He said, "You have a demon inside you."

I laughed and drank some more of my beer. Told him I was drinking even now.

"But can you do me a favor?" he asked. "Just for the next few minutes, can you put the beer down?"

"Yeah, pastor, I'll put it down," I said, but I never did.

"I just want to pray, and if it doesn't change, fine, go back to doing what you were doing. Go kill yourself. Do whatever you want to do, but I need your attention," he said.

"I'm listening," I said.

He started praying. He prayed like I've never heard anyone pray in my life. My whole life changed right there and then. I fell to the floor, I passed out, and I heard this faint voice saying, "Thomas wake up," and I heard this clapping. "Thomas, are you here? Are you with me? Are you here? Can you hear me?"

I just felt this sort of evilness and anger. The desire to drink and do drugs left. It just left, and I woke up, and I swear before God I was sober and clean. I was shaking, and I was crying, and I said, "Yes, I'm here pastor, I'm here."

"How do you feel?" he asked.

"Brand new, Pastor. I don't know what happened."

"It's God. It's God," he said. "I want you to just thank God right now."

I just started thanking God, thanking him. Pastor Ernie said good-bye, telling me he would see me in church on Sunday because he had a plane to catch. For some reason now, I felt so awake. I was concerned he would be late for his plane, and he said not to worry and hung up.

For the first time, I felt a quiet feeling within me. There were no voices telling me that my life was inadequate, that

I had nothing. For the first time it was just me controlling my thoughts. I could tell this time my life would change because I initiated the change. No outside forces made me do it. It came from within and that never happened before.

My friend was coming in the door with the beer. I took my beers, I dumped them down the sink, and he was confused. I told him I was done with this lifestyle and that I was going home to my wife and my kids. From that day I did not touch alcohol again.

I drove home. I was not drunk, but I was hysterical. I felt so much peace and joy. I felt beside myself. I was jumping up and down while driving. The car was swerving, and suddenly I saw lights behind me. A cop pulled me over.

She couldn't smell any alcohol on me. She asked, "what's so exciting?"

I said, "I'm clean; I'm clean. I'm going home to my wife and kids."

She knew me because she had arrested me before. She escorted me to my house. She asked my wife if she wanted me there, and my wife said yes. We hugged and kissed and embraced. I hugged my kids. I told her how I felt different, how things would change this time. I could see my wife looked hopeful but not convinced, which made sense given the fact that I had lied so many times.

Something happens when you get out of a dark place. Suddenly the world looks clear. For the first time I actually looked at her, with new eyes, a woman whom I tricked into being with me without loving her, a woman who gave birth to my kids and was raising them alone while dealing with me. I saw my mother in her. A woman who despite her circumstances loved her kids and tried her best to care for them. That day was bittersweet because I felt like I just survived a hurricane. I was happy to be alive, but now I was able to go outside myself and see all the damage that was done. I didn't know if it could be repaired.

I went to church that Sunday, and I saw the pastor there. His back was turned, and I just picked him up and swung him around. I said, "Oh my God, I love you so much. Thank you, thank you, thank you."

He said, "Don't thank me. Thank Jesus, thank God."

I said, "Oh my God, how did that happen? What happened and everything?"

He said, "We're in church; we're in church. We'll talk later. I have classes that I teach."

"I'm going," I said. I saw his son and grabbed his son, and I thanked him for sharing his father with me.

He knew what happened, and he said they were all praying for me.

I said, "I was drunk, and now I'm not, and I don't want no drugs, and I don't want to cheat, and I just want to straighten my life and everything."

He said they could teach me to do all that now that I was ready to listen and learn. I stayed for the church service. I talked afterward with the pastor, and I started taking classes. I opened my mind and heart to everything he had to teach me, and I sat under his feet for eight years.

CHAPTER 9

Out of Sync

I still had the drive for money and business, so a few months into being sober, I started expanding and franchising my business. I went to Boston and tried building my business up with more people. Bigger businesses, bigger territory. I felt like my life was starting to shape up on the business side. However, at home, I continued to struggle with my wife. Denise was happy about me being sober, but she had a hard time letting go of the past. She constantly reminded me of all the wrong I did, so I was still looking for sex and acceptance from other women. I still cheated, and every time I did, she still took me back. She once told me that she will always love me and takes me back because she spent half her life with me. We met with the pastor for counseling, but it wasn't working. She felt like she didn't need to change anything. She continued to deny responsibility and blame me for every issue in our relationship, which just escalated the problem.

One weekend I was coming back home from the city. I called her and told her I was coming home because I wanted to see her and the kids. Her voice was very cold and stern. She told me not to bother. I know we were having problems, so this didn't surprise me. Before I could get a word in to calm her down, she explained she was going to leave me and wanted a divorce.

I stopped in the middle of the highway. A dark heavy feeling came over me, and before I knew it the old Thomas took over my mouth. "What do you mean, you want a divorce? What the fuck are you talking about? I have been busting my ass. I got clean. I'm not drinking any more. Denise, I can't believe you're doing this. You're saying good-bye to me."

She said she found somebody else. I was angry and hurt. I was about to change my whole life, and my whole world had just caved in again. The natural thought was that she had already been seeing this guy while I was drinking and doing drugs.

I had a Jaguar, an XJ6. I loved that car. It symbolized that I was moving forward in life, but now I didn't care what happened to the car. I sped up. I did about ninety miles. When I got home, I got out of the car. The guy was there. I took a club, and I said, "Get the fuck away from my wife. I'm going to beat the fuck out of you. I'm going to kill you," and he ran.

Some people were there, some friends, my daughter's boyfriends and stuff, and they were holding me back to stop me. If it wasn't for them, I would've ended up back in jail, and this time there would be no sad stories about me not being in my right mind because I wasn't under the influence.

He got in his truck, and he left.

I said, "Fuck you, bitch! Fuck you, whore, you slut. You're nothing but a slut."

I took off and went back to Boston stayed at a friend's house. I went through a deep depression, and this time it was the most pain I ever felt, because before I would at least numb the feelings with drugs and alcohol. Now I had to deal with emotions like everyone else. I had to stay in the reality of what was going on without any place to hide. I can't say I didn't think about drinking, but I knew that wouldn't solve anything. I knew that once the alcohol wore out, the problem would still be there, and that drinking would make it worse. This time, I was learning how to explore my feelings and communicate with others, to allow them to help me.

Denise took me to court. I lost the house and was told to pay child support. Upset, I told the judge he didn't need to tell me to take care of my kids. Denise lost her car, and I lost my car, and they granted us a divorce.

The thing is, when you have so much connection with someone, you grow dependent. Although Denise was angry at me for the past and I was angry at her for her unwillingness to change, our history kept bringing us back to each other. We continued to be intimate, and I moved back in with her. I asked her to marry me again, and when we went to counseling, it was obvious that nothing had changed. We both had the same argument and she was unwilling to make any changes.

It became obvious to me that we would never see eye to eye. Our past together would always be a shadow in our relationship. At that point, I realized that if I continued to put so much effort into a relationship that was bringing me down, I was just holding myself back from becoming a better person. I decided to focus all my attention on self-improvement instead. I was meeting with ,an elder from the church. I was meeting with Don, my lifelong friend and beautiful man of God. I searched for people who fed into my life principles. I tried to fill the gaps of knowledge that were left by my previous lifestyle. I learned life skills that helped me deal with anger and the feelings that I would usually drown with alcohol and drugs. I was basically on my own for quite a while as I built the marketing business

CHAPTER 10

Strength in Layers

As humans, we have many layers, and my past makes some of my layers rough. Movies have us believe that one event turns your life around and that you will have a happy ending, but life is not a movie. That night when I gave myself to God and left alcohol and drugs behind me was a huge turning point in my life. However, there is so much more in me that I need to work on, and every day I strive to become a better person. I am aware that I need to modify my mentality in regards to some aspects of my life, yet just like the drugs, until I am open to change, it won't happen. As I continue my journey, I have relied on many people to help me become the man I one day hope to be. To them I am eternally grateful.

BUSINESS

I ran into a snag. My business started sinking, and I needed help. I had used the skills I learned in the streets to get the business running, but I never learned how to manage money or how to make money grow. I find it so strange that people do not teach their children how to manage money. We are supposed to want to learn how to work, but we are not given adequate instruction on how to build wealth.

I knew there was a gap in my mentality about money. My goal was to fill that gap with knowledge from someone who didn't only teach about wealth, but built it himself. I called the headquarters of the business. They led me to a man, a tremendous powerful man whom I respect and love, from Andover, Massachusetts.

I went to this man's business meeting, and he talked about how to go from a penny to millions of dollars. He talked about the flow of money. He talked about how money worked, how finances work, debt and getting out of debt, how money flows from someone else's pocket to your pocket. I was just listening and taking notes after notes. I must have written a book that day. The meeting was over. I went up to the man and told him that I needed someone to help lead my business team.

He said, "You lead them." He shook my hand, got my information and started helping me develop a business mindset. He gave me books, suggested CDs for me to listen to, and taught me how to make my money work for me and how to beat the "worker bee" mentality.

I left my job and got into real estate. I started renting apartments and selling cars. I got into finances; I started building business after business all thanks to the fact that I was able to find a mentor willing to share all his knowledge.

I must say that the real change began when I started giving back. That's when my fortune started to grow. I became a minister. I am now working on my sixth business, a subcontracting company. I believe in paying it forward. I believe there are a lot of people in this world who have been hurt, who have been beaten and who have been left out in the cold. But I know, deep down inside, every single person has something to give, something to offer, and I am using my experience as a base to running this new venture. I now am able to tell my team, "If I can do it, you can do it!"

MY CHILDREN

With God in my life, my life has changed a lot. I am proud of my five beautiful children and eight grandchildren. My kids are now adults, they're all working, and they all have children of their own. I see now that I wasn't a good father; I have apologized to my children both publicly and together as a family. I know I cannot turn back time, but I have tried to make my amends by being there for them now.

They all have their own issues, and I'm sure I'm to blame for a lot of them. I do feel like they all turned out well considering what I put them through. Three of my children have graduated from high school and four are working. It fills me with joy to see the way that they are raising their own children, to know that the alcohol and physical abuse that happened for generations in my family will stop with me.

We now celebrate the holidays together, and I see them quite frequently. They are the driving force for everything I do. It gives me peace that I will be able to leave them and my grandkids the means to have a comfortable life. What I am the most proud of is how they have been involved in my current business affairs. My son and I used to be distant, and he is now taking part in my subcontracting business. I know that words do not erase what I have done, but I am once again making an apology to my children. I am very sorry that I wasn't the dad that you all needed me to be, and I pray that you will forgive me and do much better by your children. It breaks my heart to know that I wasn't what you needed as a father, but I am always here now and forever. Kids are our greatest gifts from God, and we should learn to treasure them as such and remember that we are the managers of those kids, and we better do the best we can even if that means we have to change some things about ourselves first.

LOVE LIFE

Relationships are difficult enough in normal circumstances. You meet someone you are attracted to, fall in love, and then you try to spend your life with her. You try to keep that connection even though you both have undoubtedly changed.

Denise and I did not marry under normal circumstances. There were no butterflies and no getting to know each other. There was just struggle. Denise is a dedicated mother and grandmother and that's what I love about her. Most women would've walked out of my life and left me to struggle on my own. Denise stuck with me through the most turbulent times. She always tried to be there and love me even when I did not love myself.

I remember the night after I had spent three days drinking, doing drugs, and being with other women. When I finally came to my senses and went back home, she opened the door and her heart to me. Life, however, is not a fairy tale, and we did not live happily ever after. Denise and I were never able to pick up on our romantic relationship.

In fact, up until the most recent months, I have had girlfriends such as one named Tiffany. Denise knows about them, and she and I are really good friends. However, I have to let God bring to me the woman he wants me to be with. I'll tell you that when you play around and you have time to think, you start to realize that you may end up alone. That isn't always bad when you really have a personal relationship with Jesus Christ! I just love to be loved with high expectations of commitment and loyalty. I need someone who can be dedicated to me and support what I'm doing for the future of others. Denise knows who I've become and is struggling to turn into the woman I need her to be. Now that God has cleaned me up and yet is still working on me, I don't know if things with Denise will ever work out. Maybe God has someone else in store for me or maybe I will end up what I fear most—alone. When you find that special person in your life who can handle the good and the bad, and that person shares your vision, that's the person you don't let go of. Remember you never get to go back in time and have do-overs.

MY PARENTS

I think about my mother often because she's part of my motivation. She passed away before my father. They died two and a half months apart. I really hated what I did; I didn't want to let my mother down. My father I didn't care about as much; I didn't get along with him. My mother was the protector when my father tried to beat us. She was so quiet, but she loved her kids, and she made sure we had clothes on our backs even if it was hand-me-downs. She made sure we could eat.

I don't know how she did that, but she made food appear. She was just the heart and soul of that family; she stayed married to my father for fifty-eight years, through all the abuse, through all the drinking, him never showing up at home. She stayed there, just a strong woman. To this day, I've never ever met anyone like this woman. I never have. She's amazing.

I believe that her character is now coming out in me. She used to like Sam Cook, and there's a song called "I'll Always Love My Mamma." I used to sing that to my mother. She was very sick. She couldn't get up much in the last couple of days. I would go to the couch, and she'd be on the couch laying there. I'd get on the floor, and I'd hold her by the hand, and I'd start singing "I'll always love my mamma."

She said, "I know you will son." She touched my face. I miss my parents both very much, and I think now they're both looking down on me. I can just imagine them dancing together, and my mother's big smile. She's the one I want to please the most and still do to this day.

PERSONAL GROWTH AND MENTORSHIP

During my lifetime, I have been inexplicably lucky when it comes to finding people to support and mentor me. Pastor

Ernie says, "When the student is ready, the teacher will appear."

The more I open my mind and my heart to the lessons others have shared, the more success I seem to have. I am now a firm believer that it's essential to surround yourself with people who have walked the path you want to walk. Pastor Deryck, a strong family man, is someone I've come to respect a lot. He's been very instrumental in changing my life. Through that church and through him, I met his father, Pastor Ernest Frye, a man of integrity, a man of righteousness and boldness, a man who also plugged into my life a lot of wisdom and discipline.

Pastor Ernie is an admirable man. He started that church with nineteen other people, and it has grown to, well, more than 1,500 people and 7 satellite churches. There is also a ministry over in Dominican Republic. Many people know him worldwide. He's got a book out, CDs, everything. The man has done tremendously well, and I respect him highly. He was like that father for me. He introduced me to Dr. Ene Ette from Africa, who is a very strong man, a family man , a man of integrity, a man of righteousness and boldness, a man who also plugged into my life a lot of wisdom and discipline and teachings. Another mentor of mine is C. E.. With him, I've been learning about investments and finances. Mr. E. came to my rescue quite a bit, and I love him for that. All these men had one thing in common; they were very strong about what they meant, and if you didn't do it, you were left to yourself until you were ready. They helped me, and they nurtured me. They gave me books to read, passages from the Bible, particularly Proverbs, which I still read daily. There is a lot of wisdom in the Bible, particularly in Proverbs, and they are helping to mold and shape my life into what I'm becoming. All these men taught me how to be responsible, disciplined and how to mean what you say, and say what you mean. How to be gentle, how to be understanding, how to listen, how to take my time. How to grow and let God have control over my life, every single one of them. They continue to this day to be a part of my life.

I believe that every single person on this planet is a gift to someone else. If I could say anything at this point in time in my life, it would be, "Don't ever, ever, ever let anyone steal your dream. Don't ever let anyone tell you that you can't do something, period. Ever! Second, whatever it is that you believe you can do, that you have deep down in your soul even if people have tried to shut you down, I would say you bring it out, and you get started. Lastly, don't ever stop until you get it, because you have a special gift you are meant to share with the world, and nobody else is you so, nobody else has that gift."

I would say I thank God that he saved my life. It has been more than twelve years since the night when I gave up alcohol. I've not had drugs. I do have a girlfriend now. I'm very good friends with Denise. I have eight grandchildren. I have six businesses that I run. I have great friends. A great life with God, and to Him is all the glory.

Dr. Kenneth Christian, in his book, Your Own Worst Enemy, describes people he calls, "High Potential Underachievers," or "HPUAs." Dr. Christian writes, that self-defeating habits and mediocre expectations, and efforts toward goals are commonplace. There are tens of millions of dancers who don't dance, writers who don't write, athletes who quit, singers who never sing a note, preachers who won't preach, and gifted people who do nothing with their talent. They are everywhere. In boardrooms and bedrooms, in faculty lounges, from homeless to the prisons from shelters to nut houses, from athletic fields to medical schools. In every age group, in every human activity across every racial, ethnic and socioeconomic group, people achieve less than they could or abandon what they want to pursue.

Team Excel is the answer. Team Excel was founded by God , and given charge by me. To help people help themselves and to exploit the talent that is hidden within each and every one of us. "To reach for the stars and then go beyond that." We each have an assignment here on the earth, but it's being wasted. Let's not waste it anymore, and let us at Team Excel help you to reach your highest potential." Some people just need a hand up, not a hand out." Team Excel was founded on the premise to unwrap peoples' greatest potential, and to help them achieve whatever it is that they want to achieve without the government involvement. We train and develop you to be your very best! We invest in you with our time, money, blood, sweat and tears. No matter where you are in your life, you can and must do much better because you deserve it, and others deserve to be blessed by you and what you have to offer. But the number one factor is to get started today. Now!

THOMAS BLANDFORD

To contact Thomas Blandford about Team Excel, or to have him come speak to your school, group, church or organization, just send an email to: *blandfordassociates17@ rocketmail.com* or call the office 24 hours a day at (508) 298-2361, and leave a message when you call, and you will get a call back right away.

ABOUT THE AUTHOR

Thomas Blandford, along with many other ventures, is a dynamic entrepreneur, business man, minister, motivational speaker, and writer. Born in upstate New York, to an alcoholic father and an ill mother, the middle child of ten was handed off to an aunt to be raised in Harlem. After his first taste of violence at the age of six, he began his life of drug and alcohol abuse, prostitution and trouble with the Law. His behavior got him kicked out of his home at the age of fifteen. Homeless, he ventured to Massachusetts where he continued his life of addiction and violence. A failed marriage and multiple suicide attempts later, Thomas used the skills previously learned from drug selling, pimping, the streets, and his mentors he met along the way, to start his own business. Although business wise he began to succeed, his addiction continued to take over his life. One night when he was at his lowest point Thomas reached out to a pastor that helped him with the obstacles that were holding him down in life. With the help from his pastor and mentors, Thomas has found strength, guidance, and love to not only overcome his addictions, but also to be successful in all aspects of his life. He is now a man of God and a successful businessman. He is the owner of Blandford Associates, and runs a marketing company called Team Excel, which helps the disenfranchised.